Contents

Meet the farm dogs

Woof! Woof!

There's no time to rest.

Dogs have many jobs

on the farm.

Most farm dogs are large breeds.

They can weigh 36 kilogrammes

(80 pounds) or more.

Shepherds, collies and terriers

make good farm dogs.

But many farm dogs are

a mix of more than one breed.

They are called mongrels.

On the farm

Border collies herd sheep.

The dogs guide the grazing flock

back to the barn.

Australian cattle dogs move

cows across pastures.

The dogs nip the heels

of slower cows.

Guard dogs protect

the farm. They make sure foxes

don't kill the chickens.

Rats and mice can scare horses

and get into grain stores.

Terriers chase rodents

out of barns.

Looking after farm dogs

Farm dogs should see a vet once

a year. Dogs need vaccinations

against diseases, such as rabies.

Rabies can be spread through

bites from other animals.

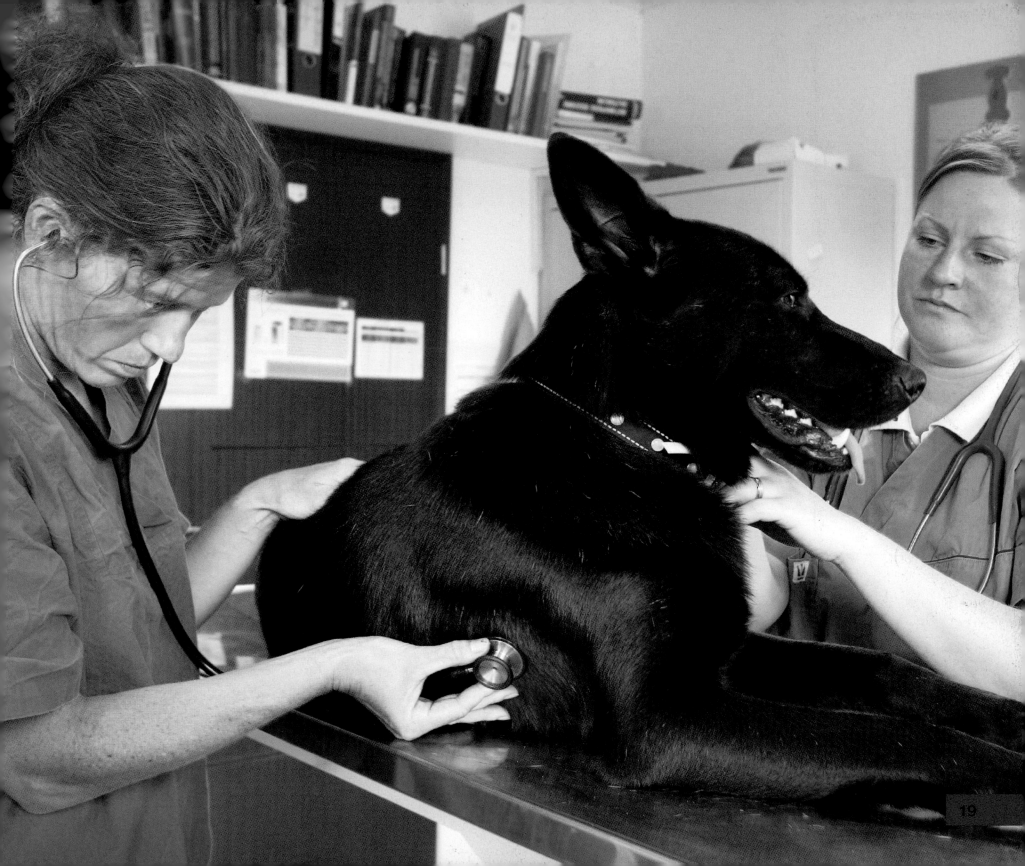

Time to rest

It's been a long day

on the farm. Tired dogs

rest in the barn.

Some dogs sleep inside

the farmhouse with their owners.

Glossary

breed certain kind of animal within an animal group

collie breed of thick-coated dog used to herd sheep or cows

flock group of sheep; members of flocks live, travel and eat together

grain store large container that holds grain such as corn, wheat or oats

herd bring together into a large group

pasture land where farm animals eat grass and exercise

rabies a deadly disease that people and animals can get from the bite of an infected animal

terrier any of several breeds of small, lively dogs that were first bred for hunting small animals that live in burrows

vaccination an injection that protects animals from a disease

Read more

Dogs (Animal Abilities), Charlotte Guillain (Raintree, 2013)

Dogs (Little Scientist), Martha E. H. Rustad (Capstone Press, 2015)

Farm Animals (Say & Point Picture Book), Nicola Tuxworth (Armadillo Books, 2015)

Websites

discoverykids.com/category/animals/
Learn facts about animals and check out photos of all sorts of animals on this website.

kids.nationalgeographic.com/animals
Search for different sorts of animals and learn where they live, what they eat and more.

Index

Raintree is an imprint of Capstone Global Library Limited, a company incorporated in England and Wales having its registered office at 264 Banbury Road, Oxford, OX2 7DY – Registered company number: 6695582

www.raintree.co.uk
myorders@raintree.co.uk

Text © Capstone Global Library Limited 2016
The moral rights of the proprietor have been asserted.

Edited by Erika L. Shores
Designed by Ashlee Suker
Picture research by Marcie Spence
Production by Eric Manske

ISBN 978 1 4747 1908 2 (hardback)
20 19 18 17 16
10 9 8 7 6 5 4 3 2 1

ISBN 978 1 4747 1915 5 (paperback)
21 20 19 18 17
10 9 8 7 6 5 4 3 2 1

Photo Credits
Alamy: inga spence, 15; Fiona Green Animal Photography, 7; Getty Images: Jeffrey L. Jaquish ZingPix.com, 13; iStockphoto: dageldog, 5, happyborder, cover, 1, Jan-Otto, 19, Photomorphic, 11, ShashaFoxWalters, 21; Shutterstock: djets, design element, Joy Brown, 17, yurra, 9

We would like to thank Gail Saunders-Smith, PhD, and Dr. Celina Johnson for their invaluable help in the preparation of this book.

Every effort has been made to contact copyright holders of material reproduced in this book. Any omissions will be rectified in subsequent printings if notice is given to the publisher.

All the internet addresses (URLs) given in this book were valid at the time of going to press. However, due to the dynamic nature of the internet, some addresses may have changed, or sites may have changed or ceased to exist since publication. While the author and publisher regret any inconvenience this may cause readers, no responsibility for any such changes can be accepted by either the author or the publisher.

This book describes and illustrates farm dogs. The images support early readers in understanding the text. The repetition of words and phrases helps early readers learn new words. This book also introduces early readers to subject-specific vocabulary which is defined in the Glossary section. Early readers may need assistance to read some words and to use the Table of contents, Glossary, Read more, Internet sites and Index sections of the book.

Printed and bound in China.

FARM ANIMALS

FARM DOGS

by Kathryn Clay

raintree

a Capstone company — publishers for children